A Special Thank You!

As a special thank you for your book purchase, please log onto the following link below to download your free colouring book to print and enjoy!

Link:
www.amazinglycoolbooks.com/specialthankyou

Copyright © 2020 Natalie Murray

Grow Up And Be Great!
www.amazinglycoolbooks.com

The moral right of the author has been asserted.

All rights reserved. No part of this publication may be reproduced, stored in a retrieval system, or transmitted, in any form or by any means, electronic, mechanical, photocopying, recording, or otherwise, without prior written permission from the publisher.

Illustration by Sarah-Leigh Wills.
www.happydesigner.co.uk

DMJ Publishing
www.dmjpublishing.co.uk

Grow Up And Be Great!

Written by
Natalie Murray

Illustrations by
Happydesigner

I like thinking of others, not just myself.
I like finding different ways to help
I like asking many questions: when, who,
why, how, and what?
That means I like learning so I will learn a lot!

I like taking care of people
when they are hurt.
Maybe one day I will be
a doctor or a nurse!

I like building things and fixing things
and finding out how they work.
I like using my hands.
Although I don't say many words.

I like puzzles and problems
and figuring things out.
I like using my brain without a doubt.

I like giving. It makes me happy
when others smile.
Then we smile together
and have a good time

I like telling lots of jokes.
And making others feel great.
When we are happy, we have lots of fun,
And I've got lots of mates.

I like cheering people up
Especially when they are sad.
We can talk together, then they will feel better
And that makes me glad.

Some of us like doing things.
Some of us like making things.
Some of us like fixing, arranging,
and inventing things.

Some of us like helping, caring,
and listening to people.
We are all wonderful and unique,
That's what makes us a blessing to others,
which is what the world needs!

Other books in the series:

Have you got all 4?

www. amazinglycoolbooks.com

www.ingramcontent.com/pod-product-compliance
Lightning Source LLC
Chambersburg PA
CBHW081400080526
44588CB00016B/2557